IMAGES
of America

HARBOR
COUNTRY

IMAGES
of America

HARBOR
COUNTRY

Robert and RoseAnna Mueller

ARCADIA
PUBLISHING

Published by Arcadia Publishing
Charleston, South Carolina

Library of Congress Catalog Card Number: 2002114114

For all general information contact Arcadia Publishing at:
Telephone 843-853-2070
Fax 843-853-0044
E-mail sales@arcadiapublishing.com
For customer service and orders:
Toll-Free 1-888-313-2665

Visit us on the Internet at www.arcadiapublishing.com

CONTENTS

ACKNOWLEDGMENTS

The following publications were especially useful in our research for this book, and we recommend them to anyone who would like to learn more about Harbor Country's history:

   Burgh, Robert. *The Region of Three Oaks*. Three Oaks, Michigan: The Edward K. Warren Foundation, 1939.
   Hunt, Mary and Don. *Hunt's Guide to West Michigan*. Waterloo, Michigan: Midwestern Guides, 1990.
   Kissman, Nadra. *The New Buffalo Story 1834–1976*. The New Buffalo Area Bicentennial Committee, 1976.
   Sweeney, Jeanne. *A Short History of the Village of Grand Beach*. Privately published, 1969.
   Multiple authors. *Centennial History of Lakeside*. Lakeside, Michigan: The Village of Lakeside Association Inc., 1974.
   Red Arrow Review. May, June, July 1993, and summer, 1994.
   The History of Michiana, Michigan. Village of Michiana, 1996.

In addition, several individuals and organizations provided invaluable advice and the loan of personal photos used in this book. Sue Harsch of the Harbor Country Chamber of Commerce put us in touch with many photo sources. The Chamber shares quarters with the New Buffalo Railroad Museum—well worth a visit, incidentally—which displays many early photos, some of them loaned to us by their owner, Nadra Kissman of Nadra K Real Estate in New Buffalo.

Ms. Kissman, a descendant of the Wilkinson family, early Lakeside settlers, also operates the Wilkinson Museum on Red Arrow Highway. The museum occupies the ground floor of the old Wilkinson trading post, one of Lakeside's earliest buildings. It, too, is worth a visit. Many of the early photos of Lakeside in this book came from the museum.

Ruth Magdzinski, a long-time Lakeside resident and owner of Lakeside Country Shores Realty, loaned us some photos of the area and put us in touch with the owners of other photo collections. Robert Rosenbaum of Union Pier gave us access to his wonderful collection of early postcards from the area, a great many of which are reproduced in this volume.

New Buffalo Librarian Bonnie Kliss provided advice and loaned us photos from the library's collection. Sherri and Lee Waddle, owners of Hannah's Restaurant in New Buffalo, were kind enough to temporarily remove some of the photos that decorate their restaurant so that we could scan them.

The Village of Grand Beach gave us access to a group of scrapbooks compiled by Jantena Jensen and Sidney Bohling Hoover. The scrapbooks contain many photos and early documents. Bryan Volstorf, who manages the Three Oaks Spokes bicycle club and its Bicycle Museum, let us borrow photos of the Apple Cider Century, an annual bicycle tour the group sponsors.

Harry B. Rosenberg, a long-time summer resident of Michiana, loaned us some family photos that date from Michiana's early days. Barry Patejdl of the Sawyer Garden Center let us scan some early images of Harbert and Sawyer from his personal collection.

6

INTRODUCTION

A *New York Times* travel writer wrote several years ago, "What the Hamptons are to New York and Cape Cod is to Boston, Harbor Country is to Chicago." Indeed, some see similarities between the tidy cottages of the area's summer residents and those of New England resorts, or the growing number of lakeside mansions with those of Long Island's southeastern shore.

But despite escalating property values and pricey restaurants and shops, the area has managed to retain an artless, Mayberryesque quality, especially evident at local events like Three Oaks' Flag Day Parade: a wistful, old-fashioned look and feel, evocative of family vacations and weekends at Grandma's cottage a half-century ago. It's a quality that's managed to defy most attempts (and there have been many) to bring manufactured trendiness to the area.

Harbor Country—a name created in the 1980s by the area's Chamber of Commerce—includes seven villages along 14 miles of Lake Michigan shoreline, starting with woodsy Michiana, on the Michigan/Indiana state line, and ending at Sawyer, just south of spectacular Warren Dunes State Park. As though to remind visitors that there are inland sights worth seeing, an eighth community, Three Oaks—about six miles east of the shoreline—also is included.

Almost no one who visits or lives in the area calls it Harbor Country, but there is a sort of unity, centered on New Buffalo's main street and yacht harbor, that nearly everyone recognizes. Sometimes the term "Harbor Country" gets stretched to include the nearby resort areas of Indiana—Long Beach and Sheridan Beach, even Michigan City—and the towns north of Sawyer all the way up to the southern fringes of St. Joseph. For this book, however, we have followed the Chamber's definition.

On a summer weekend, the population of New Buffalo easily quadruples, causing tie-ups at the town's one traffic light and pushing waiting times at popular restaurants above an hour. The area's public beaches are packed, and ski boats and wave runners buzz by a hundred yards offshore. There are antique shops to explore, produce markets and orchards for fresh Michigan berries and apples, quiet bed-and-breakfasts with broad porches and, sometimes, stretches of private beach.

It almost seems predestined that this little strip of shoreline would become a popular vacation spot. Chicago is just an hour and a half away, a sensible drive for a weekend visit or even a day trip. Indianapolis and Detroit send some regular visitors to the area. Except for occasional periods when the lake is high, the beaches are sandy and wide, and the country roads that run inland from them seem made for wandering.

But with two exceptions—Michiana and Grand Beach—none of Harbor Country's towns started out with tourism in mind. In fact, the towns of Harbor Country have gone through boom-and-bust cycles, and at various times even their survival has been in doubt.

La Salle Takes a Look, Moves On

The earliest Europeans to visit the area around Harbor Country and leave a record were a group of French explorers under the command of Robert Cavalier Sieur de la Salle. La Salle was looking for a way to reach the Pacific by way of the Great Lakes and inland rivers, particularly the Mississippi, which Jacques Marquette and Louis Joliet had reached several years earlier.

Already a well-known explorer when he began his trip down the Mississippi, La Salle started out from Niagara in 1679 in a small ship, and arrived at the French settlement in Green Bay, Wisconsin later the same year. From there, he sent the ship, the *Griffon*, now loaded with furs, back to Niagara and agreed to meet it at the mouth of the St. Joseph River. La Salle then followed the shoreline of Lake Michigan, past Harbor Country, to the St. Joseph.

The *Griffon* was never heard from again. La Salle built a small fort, which he called Fort des Miamis, at present-day St. Joseph. He left a small group to garrison the fort and began his trip downriver. La Salle reached the Gulf of Mexico in 1682, and claimed the entire Mississippi basin, which he named Louisiana after Louis XIV, for France. When he returned to Fort des Miamis, La Salle found it abandoned and in ruins.

Not far from the portage from the St. Joseph River to the Kankakee, near present-day Niles, the French built another fort, Fort St. Joseph, in 1691. That fort was abandoned around 1700, but a mission and trading post stayed on, and so, briefly, did the name.

La Salle was an explorer and builder of forts, and he had no interest in settling the lands he discovered. It was nearly 150 years before the land around Harbor Country attracted its first permanent settlers. The treaty that ended the Revolutionary War ceded the Great Lakes states to the United States, but the British were reluctant losers, and, along with Indian allies, harassed American settlements in the Northwest Territories. Eventually, that—along with attacks on American shipping—led to the War of 1812. Even after that war ended, in 1814, and Berrien County (including Harbor Country) was surveyed in 1829, threats, real or imagined, from hostile Indians kept settlers away.

The Indian issue was resolved in 1830 by the Indian Removal Act. The Act forced the Indians to move out of the Lake Michigan area to Iowa. Their brief, poorly-organized attempt to regain their land around the lake in 1835, called Blackhawk's War, was quickly put down.

It's tempting to view the early settlers of Harbor Country as rugged explorers, along the lines of Daniel Boone or Davy Crockett. In fact, Harbor Country's communities developed rather late, compared to those in the surrounding area. The oldest community, New Buffalo, was incorporated in 1836. By then, Michigan City and Niles (then called Bertrand) were thriving communities, and across the lake, Chicago's phenomenal growth was already underway. (The city had a population of nearly 4,000 when it was incorporated in 1837.) Commercial traffic on the St. Joseph River began as early as 1829, and by 1837, there was passenger service via steamship between Chicago and New Buffalo.

One reason most of Harbor Country's towns developed late was that they were somewhat inaccessible. While the St. Joseph was navigable as far as South Bend, it was impossible to travel down New Buffalo's river, the Galien, more than a few miles inland without running into snags and sand bars. Michigan's territorial government authorized a highway, later called M-11, between St. Joseph and Michigan City in 1833, but for years afterward, only the stretch between New Buffalo and the Indiana state line was reliable. (Portions of Lakeshore Road, U.S. 12 and Old Grand Beach Road follow M-11's route, which in turn followed an old Indian trail.) It wasn't until the railroads arrived in the late 1840s, and lumbermen built piers into the lake in the 1850s and 1860s, that much of Harbor Country became accessible.

Furthermore, at first there wasn't much reason to settle Harbor Country. A great deal of the land around Harbor Country was swampy and heavily forested. That made it undesirable for farming—which, apart from land speculation, was the main occupation of settlers from New England, upstate New York, and the South. The swamps bred mosquitoes, and there were periodic outbreaks of malaria.

But the forests yielded lumber, and as Chicago and other cities on the lake grew, entrepreneurs among the early settlers, along with some newcomers, developed Harbor Country's first real industry: harvesting timber, milling it into lumber, and shipping it across the lake from piers built out from the shoreline.

By the late 1800s, however, the timber was largely gone and the piers fell into ruin. The railroad, which had brought a few brief years of prosperity to New Buffalo (when it was the terminus of the Michigan Central line), left it nearly a ghost town after 1853 when tracks were laid through to Chicago. With the forests gone, the local population turned to fruit and vegetable farming. Orchards, berry farms, and vineyards are still common along the country roads that run away from the lake.

Harbor Country's economy was revitalized around the turn of the 20th century, when tourists from Chicago began discovering the area's beaches. Enterprising farmers turned lakeside properties into resorts. Ethnic and religious groups built summer camps and lodges. New resort communities were formed, and Chicago's famous—and infamous—flocked to the area. Carl Sandburg had a place in Harbert, where he raised goats. Hull House founder Jane Addams rented a cottage in Lakeside, and Al Capone was a frequent visitor to the same town. Chicago Mayor Anton Cermak and Olympic hero Jesse Owens had summer homes in Union Pier, and Cermak's eventual successor, Richard Daley, settled his family in Grand Beach. Restaurants, night clubs, and taverns sprung up to serve the summer visitors.

After World War II, however, Harbor Country's tourist boom went bust. Cheap airfares and better highways took many Chicagoans further afield for vacations; the advent of air conditioning made Chicago's summers bearable, and kept other visitors home. Some families held onto summer homes, but many were abandoned and fell into disrepair. Restaurants that had served visitors for decades went out of business, and resorts struggled to stay afloat.

This image depicts Red Arrow Highway in the 1930s. Along with U.S. 12, of which Red Arrow is an extension, the highway has been bringing visitors to Harbor Country for many decades.

9

HARBOR COUNTRY'S COMEBACK

Then, in the mid-1970s, things began to turn around. Many credit the creation of New Buffalo's yacht harbor, finished in 1975, for the area's renaissance. Completion of I-94, five years earlier, probably played a role as well. Some say overdevelopment of Wisconsin's resort towns sent Chicagoans looking for unspoiled, affordable waterfront. In any case, a new generation of weekenders and summer vacationers discovered the towns of Harbor Country. Rundown cottages and inns changed hands for a song, and were renovated or replaced by their new owners. Property values shot up, new restaurants opened, and Harbor Country was back in business.

This book is meant to be a brief history of Harbor Country, told mostly through images from the late 19th through the mid-20th century. It is by no means the complete story of the area—for that, we recommend the volumes listed in the acknowledgements section—but we hope it will give visitors, summer residents, and year-round citizens at least a glimpse of the area's past.

One

NEW BUFFALO

In November 1834, Wessel Whittaker, a Great Lakes skipper from Buffalo, New York, encountered a fierce fall storm at the southwest end of Lake Michigan. Spotting a creek at the southern end of what is now Grand Beach, he made for shore, but his ship, the *Post Boy*, ran aground and broke up.

Whittaker and his crew made it to dry land and walked to Michigan City, then a four-year-old frontier town. There they arranged for transportation to St. Joseph to report the loss of the ship. Not far north of where the *Post Boy* had foundered, Whittaker saw what he thought would make an ideal harbor—in fact, the major harbor on the southern end of Lake Michigan. A lagoon called Lake Potawatomi, about two miles from north to south and half a mile across, opened onto the lake through a channel on the south end of a long sandbar. The Galien River emptied into the lagoon at its north end. After taking care of his business in St. Joseph, Whittaker rushed down to Kalamazoo and began buying up parcels around his would-be harbor.

He then returned to Buffalo and spent the winter lining up investors and settlers for his new city, which he and his partners named New Buffalo. The following March, Whittaker and four others started out overland for the new settlement. They were soon joined by others. The first building was a log cabin on the corner of Whittaker and Merchant streets. (Henry Merchant was a manager for Jacob Barker and Nelson Willard, Whittaker's former employers and partners in the New Buffalo venture, and was also one of the first settlers.)

More buildings, including a warehouse, store, and hotel, soon followed. The settlers cut a road to a sawmill in northern Indiana for lumber to build the town. Whittaker himself bought interests in sawmills along the Galien River near New Buffalo and on State Creek, the same creek in which the *Post Boy* unsuccessfully had sought shelter a year earlier.

But while the captain dabbled in lumber and other local industry, he never lost sight of his vision of turning New Buffalo into a major port. History took another direction, however. Whittaker laid out a block called Seaman's Square and donated lots to other Great Lakes captains, in hopes of luring them to his new port. All of them sold their properties and never set foot in New Buffalo. A financial panic in 1837 sent property values plummeting, and the settlement, just two years old, went into decline.

Whittaker died broke in 1841, and his dream of making New Buffalo into a major port city died with him. By then, Lake Potawatomi had already begun silting in, thanks partly to overcutting by lumbermen, and Chicago was well on its way to becoming the pre-eminent city in the region.

The Village of New Buffalo was incorporated in 1836, but by 1840, the entire township had a population of only 123. By 1842 only two families lived in town. Nobody bothered to renew the town charter until 1869, and the village fell into the first of several periods of decline.

Then, almost by accident, New Buffalo rebounded. In 1837, the state took over a defunct railroad that aimed to link Detroit with Chicago. It got as far as Kalamazoo by 1846, but dwindling funds forced the state to sell the existing track to a group of investors that called itself the Michigan Central Railroad Company. The new company chose New Buffalo as its western terminus.

The first train rolled into town in 1849, and the sleepy village became a boomtown. Passengers and freight were offloaded onto Chicago-bound steamships from piers built out into the lake by the Michigan Central. Hotels, restaurants and stores thrived. Many of the passengers were German farmers headed west, but some stayed on in New Buffalo to form the town's first immigrant community.

The railroad boom ended just four years after it began. By 1853, the Michigan Central had laid tracks through to Chicago, and there was no longer any reason to stop in New Buffalo. The area retreated into farming and logging, and the village itself became a quiet rural community. One account by an early settler called it a ghost town.

New Buffalo's second renaissance started in the late 1800s, when visitors began to discover the area's potential as a resort. The beaches and quiet back roads appealed to busy Chicagoans, and the trains that rolled through the town on their way to the city began to bring passengers from Chicago to New Buffalo on the return trip.

An enterprising farmer named Isaac Smith built one of the first resorts on his lakefront property in 1893, to accommodate visitors en route to the Columbian Exposition in Chicago. Others soon joined him. New Buffalo and the area immediately surrounding it became a popular spot for religious and ethnic summer camps. In 1903, a church group opened a camp called

WESSEL WHITTAKER GOES TO WAR

In 1835, Wessel Whittaker and a group of recent New Buffalo settlers made their way to Niles to join the Michigan militia for what was probably one of the shortest and arguably the most peculiar war in American history.

In 1787, the year Britain ceded what were to become the Great Lakes states to the United States as part of the treaty that ended the Revolutionary War, the Northwest Ordinance decreed that the southern boundary of Michigan Territory would follow a line drawn due east from the southern point of Lake Michigan to Lake Erie. Thanks to a surveying error, however, the bottom tip of Lake Michigan was placed about 10 miles north of its actual location.

In 1818, Michigan's territorial governor ordered a new survey that moved the line further south to the point originally intended in 1787. By that time, however, Ohio had already claimed the mouth of the Maumee River at Lake Erie—later the port city of Toledo—which lay within the 1818 Michigan boundary. When Michigan applied for statehood in 1833, the question of the state line became a serious issue. Ohio insisted the 1787 line was correct; Michigan argued for the 1818 boundary.

When negotiations broke down in 1835, Michigan Governor Stephens T. Mason, appointed to the post by Andrew Jackson at the age of 19, ordered the militia to the disputed area to protect the territory's interests. Ohio Governor Robert Lucas responded in kind. In April of that year, both sides were ready for bloody battle, but the two armies got lost in a swamp, and neither could find the other. The federal government stepped in and ordered Michigan, as a condition of statehood, to give up the so-called Toledo Strip. In exchange, it got the Upper Peninsula. Whittaker and his band of men from New Buffalo apparently never got further than Niles.

Potawatomie Point. Two years later, the Bohemian Club of Chicago opened Camp Sokol. In 1916, the Chicago YWCA bought land south of New Buffalo Village and opened the Forest Beach Camp. Camp Tell Hai, a Jewish boys' camp, operated in the 1930s.

As other Harbor Country resorts gained steam, New Buffalo became the area's commercial center. Restaurants, taverns, hotels, and other services thrived on tourist dollars, as Chicago's rich and famous visited on weekends or bought summer houses on the beaches nearby. Roads were widened and improved, and the railroads that once brought tourists to New Buffalo were replaced by automobiles.

But just as the railroad brought boom followed by bust in the mid-19th century, the better highways that brought tourists to town in the first half of the 20th century took them beyond it by mid-century. The Interstate highway system made long-distance vacations by car practical and cheap. Air travel became more reliable and economical, and air conditioning made Chicago's tropical summers more bearable. Reasons for vacationing in Southwest Michigan dwindled as higher-profile destinations in the U.S. and abroad were suddenly accessible and affordable. Once again, New Buffalo went into decline.

A Harbor and a Highway

The village experienced a third renaissance in the 1970s. Interstate 94, completed in 1970, shortened the trip for Chicagoans, and an ambitious harbor project finished in 1975 turned tourists' heads. Enthusiastic write-ups in the Chicago and national press brought a new generation of visitors. Real estate values, depressed for decades, shot up as out-of-towners began snapping up vacation houses on or near area beaches.

Today, New Buffalo is once again the commercial center of Harbor Country's resorts, yet it remains relatively unspoiled. Shops and restaurants come and go, but the village has so far kept its small-town ambience and avoided the homogenized look that comes with chain stores and franchises. It may not be exactly what Wessel Whittaker had in mind when he stumbled on the mouth of the Galien 170 years ago, but New Buffalo has ultimately become a thriving, well-known community.

When this photo was taken in the early 1900s, boating was already a popular pastime, though New Buffalo's harbor amounted to little more than a wide spot where the Galien River entered Lake Michigan. The bridge in the background may be the one that was destroyed by the "Great Wave" of 1908—technically, a seiche caused by different atmospheric conditions on the two sides of the lake. The wave brought a 10-foot wall of water as far north as the railroad tracks at Mechanic Street.

In this pre-1908 photo, visitors headed north of the Galien River in New Buffalo walk across an old railroad trestle bridge, originally built to haul freight onto piers jutting out into Lake Michigan. The alternative was to take the train to Union Pier, then head south—a much longer walk.

The bridge destroyed by the 1908 seiche was replaced by the one shown in this photo, from about 1912. Note how much lower the river level is in this photo than in previous two.

Isaac Smith converted his 165-acre lakefront farm to a resort in 1893, to accommodate guests on their way to the Columbian Exposition in Chicago. The hotel may have been the first resort in Harbor Country. It included a 10-room main building, 10 cottages, and a ballroom.

These 1890s guests at Isaac Smith's Resort Hotel on Marquette (Riviera) Road have camped out for the day on a nearby dune. The signs read, "The gang's retreat" and "Please wipe your feet."

This postcard, from around 1909, shows a section of the old trestle bridge and an area called "Boat House Corner." The buildings on the far side of the bridge may be part of William Guhl's commercial fishing operation.

New Buffalo's beaches already were a big attraction when this turn-of-the-century photo was taken. Beachwear, however, still had a long way to go.

18

Commercial fishing was very much a part of life in the early 1900s, when this postcard was published. Pictured is the Dutch Schafer fishing crew. Schafer himself is standing in his boat.

This 1865 hand pumper was shipped across Lake Michigan to help put out the 1871 Chicago Fire. It was restored in 1959 by students at the Michigan State Reformatory. The pumper is a popular sight at local parades.

New Buffalo's first school, a one-room structure erected in the 1830s, was replaced by this building sometime before 1908. The wood frame building was destroyed by a fire in 1915.

This brick school building replaced the wood frame elementary school after 1915. Later, it served as the city hall. It was razed in the 1990s when a new city hall was built on the same site.

Construction of New Buffalo High School began in 1930. For a time, elementary grades were also housed in the building. With the recent completion of a new high school building, the old school is being turned into condominiums.

This photo shows Whittaker Avenue, New Buffalo's main street, as it appeared around 1910. The photo looks south, toward U.S. 12.

This view of Whittaker Avenue was taken around the same time as the previous photo. The brick buildings replaced wooden ones, which burned in a major fire in 1900.

Another view, looking north from the corner of Whittaker and Buffalo, shows downtown New Buffalo in the mid-1930s.

1930ˢ

Whittaker Rd. at U.S. Highway No. 12, New Buffalo, M

By the mid-1930s, the intersection of Whittaker and U.S. 12 was busy enough to require a stoplight. This photo faces north, toward the lake, and the perspective is similar to that of the previous photo. The Buffalo Cafe is on the left; Schmidt's drugstore is on the right.

The corner of Whittaker and Buffalo (U.S. 12) was home to Schmidt's drugstore for many years. The drugstore, then called the Josenhans Drug Store, burned down in the "great fire" of 1962, which also claimed several other nearby businesses. More than 200 fire fighters, some from as far away as Michigan City, helped put out the flames.

The Michigan Central Railroad depot, on Mechanic Street in New Buffalo, had the village's first running water and separate waiting rooms for men and women. This image is from a postcard postmarked 1918.

The first Catholic Church—the second church building in New Buffalo—was finished in 1858. The current church, St. Mary's of the Lake—shown here with its rectory—dates to 1936, when the 1858 building was torn down.

The First Methodist Church on South Whittaker is the oldest house of worship in town. It dates back to 1861–1862. Congregationalists, German Evangelicals, and Baptists also built early churches in New Buffalo.

Part of Harbor Country's charm lies in the fact that it has, for the most part, escaped the attention of large, national retail chains. Pictured in this 1953 photo is Heppler's grocery store on North Whittaker in New Buffalo.

By 1909, when this postcard was mailed, New Buffalo and other Harbor Country towns had begun to regard their beaches as major assets. Tourism was on the rise, and the area's economy began turning away from agriculture and toward new services for the visiting Chicagoans who were crowding into the area during the summer.

In this photo, undated but probably from the late 1920s, bathers take advantage of a sunny day on a New Buffalo beach.

Beach-goers in 1929 tested the waters at the mouth of the Galien River, which winds inland in the background.

The ruins of an early pier are still visible in this 1939 view of New Buffalo's beach. The first piers in town were built in the 1840s. Lumber was carried on horse-drawn railroad cars to steamships docked at the piers, and shipped to Chicago and other growing Great Lakes cities. Later, when New Buffalo was the terminus of the Michigan Central, the railroad ran trains up the piers, and cargo was offloaded onto steamships.

This image depicts a beach party near the Rio on the public beach at New Buffalo.

Although the Galien River is only navigable for a short distance from Lake Michigan, excursion boats, like "The Ark," pictured here, made frequent trips upriver. A note on this undated photo reads that The Ark "is nearly as full as the one of ancient fame."

This steel bridge was built over the Galien at Whittaker Street in 1914, and was replaced by the current bridge in 1975.

This image depicts a boater speeding down the Galien River in the 1940s.

With boating's popularity in Harbor Country, accidents are an unfortunately common occurrence. In this photo, Coast Guard and New Buffalo Police officers discuss the possible location of a missing boater.

In the first few decades of the 20th century, New Buffalo became home to a number of camps, often sponsored by ethnic or religious groups. Camp Sokol, founded around 1905, was one of the first and largest.

Founded by Joe Babke of the Bohemian Club of Chicago, Camp Sokol boasted it was the largest Bohemian camp in the country by 1921. In that year, it could handle 200 guests. By around 1940, when this photo was taken, tents had been replaced by tidy rows of cottages.

This is another view of Camp Sokol, from a postcard dated 1938.

The Chicago YWCA established a girls' camp called Forest Beach between New Buffalo and Grand Beach in 1916. The property had been a sanatorium, then briefly a resort, before the YWCA acquired it. In the 1990s, the camp was sold to a developer who, after a brief battle with conservationists, built summer houses and condos in the former camp.

In this photo, visitors enjoy a fall weekend at Forest Beach Camp in New Buffalo. In 1921, the camp drew more than 1,500 visitors.

Pictured here is the dining pavilion at Forest Beach.

Swimming, hiking, and sports—like this baseball game in the mid-1920s—were among the organized activities at Forest Beach Camp. Board in the 1920s cost about $7 a week.

Jackson Park, another campground resort shown in this postcard mailed in 1927, was located on U.S. 12 near the Pine Grove Cemetery.

In 1931, when this photo was taken, the Fairview Hotel was a popular stopover for visitors to New Buffalo. Built in the late 1800s, the Fairview was originally the summer home of August "Doc" Birkholz, a prominent landowner and faith healer. The Fairview later became the Little Bohemia Restaurant, and is now Hannah's Restaurant.

The Rio, a popular hotel and restaurant on New Buffalo's beach, was built in the 1930s. It was remodeled and renamed the Surf and Sand in the late 1950s, and burned down in 1959. This view of the Rio is from across the Galien River, near the current mouth of the harbor.

This is another view of the Rio hotel and restaurant, from the sand dunes of New Buffalo's beach.

As vacationers discovered New Buffalo, restaurants and other facilities were built to serve them. A popular eating place was the Buffalo Cafe on the corner of Whittaker Street and U.S. 12. The cafe advertised charcoal-broiled steaks, chicken, and seafood, and was air-conditioned.

Another popular restaurant in New Buffalo was the Calvin Grille & Red Cedar Tap Room, just down the road from the Buffalo Cafe. The site is now the parking lot for Jackson's produce market.

A forerunner of fast food restaurants, Carl's Hut on U.S. 12 offered hamburgers, home-made soup, fountain service, cigars, and candy. The restaurant opened in 1946.

Two

UNION PIER

By the late 1850s, Harbor Country's shoreline bristled with piers. Shortly after 1849, the Michigan Central Railroad built a pier in New Buffalo to offload passengers and freight onto ships bound for Chicago. John Wilkinson built his pier, for loading lumber onto schooners, in Lakeside a few years later. Others jutted into the lake at Harbert and Sawyer.

Franklin Gowdy arrived in what is now Union Pier in 1862. Along with a brother, John Gowdy, and several other local landowners, he built a sawmill and a pier in Chikaming Township that extended 600 feet into Lake Michigan. Franklin Gowdy also had a stake in a local company that made tool handles, and he grew fruit, mostly peaches, on an orchard near the lake.

Gowdy's pier, at the end of present-day Berrien Street, was connected to the timberlands and mills further inland by a horse-drawn (some accounts say mule-drawn or ox-drawn) tramway that paralleled Warren Woods Road. At the same time, he and his partners built a 130-ton schooner, the *Hawkins*, on the beach near the pier, to carry their lumber to markets in Chicago and elsewhere.

WHY "UNION" PIER?

No one seems to know exactly why the pier was called Union Pier. According to one theory, "union" was a reference to the partnership that built the pier. According to another, the pier, built during the Civil War, was patriotically named for The Union, as many towns and schools were at that time. In either case, when a post office opened in the lumber community a few years later, it was called "Union Pier," and the name stuck.

By the final decades of the 19th century, most of the forests around Union Pier had been cleared by lumbermen and replaced by farms and orchards. The pier itself, neglected through several winters, largely collapsed, and the town became a quiet farming community.

That all changed in the first years of the 20th century. A second-generation Union Pier Gowdy, Herbert, along with other family members, noted the growing popularity of the area among vacationers, and together they developed a 40-acre parcel of family land, known today as Gowdy Shores, as a summer home community.

By the 1920s, Union Pier was a booming resort town. Hotels, cabins, restaurants, dance halls, and even a casino sprang up in the village. Olympian Jesse Owens had a place in Union Pier. Chicago Mayor Anton Cermak did, too. John Dillinger was a visitor.

And, unlike some other resort towns in Harbor Country, Union Pier welcomed ethnic and religious diversity. Czechs and Bohemians were among the early permanent and summer residents. They were joined by Jewish families a few years later and, later still, by African-Americans, Lithuanians, and other eastern Europeans. One publication calls Union Pier "the United Nations of tourism."

Then, in the years following World War II, tourism collapsed, as it did in many of Harbor Country's other communities. Some second-home owners held onto their properties and a few of the town's inns kept operating, but much of Union Pier's tourist economy fell into ruin. Restaurants closed, summer cottages fell into disrepair, and as it had after the lumber boom, the village went into a shabby slumber.

By the 1970s and 1980s, however, the same forces that were revitalizing New Buffalo and Harbor Country's other resorts were being felt in Union Pier. Tumbledown cottages were bought by Chicagoans and rehabbed or replaced, and real estate values rose. Resort hotels from the 1920s were remodeled and recast as bed-and-breakfasts, and new restaurants and shops opened to replace those that were shuttered a few decades earlier. Once again, Union Pier became fashionable.

WHO WAS WHO IN 1873

An 1873 document, reprinted 10 years ago, lists the following businesses in Chikaming Township:

"A.L. Drew...Dealer in all kinds of Agricultural Impliments; also Notary Public, Justice of the Peace and Farmer. P.O. Three Oaks, Res. on Sec. 26.
R.M. Goodwin & Co....Dealers in also Manufacturer and Shippers of Hardwood Lumber and Cordwood, Give particular attention to Manufacturing Hardwood Lumber to order, We contract for and handle Rail Road Cross and Switches, Oak Planks for Street Crossing & c. and handle large quantities of Cord wood, Delivering on Dock in City of Chicago. Also, buy and Sell Timber and Farm Lands. We also keep a general and full Stock of Domestic Dry Goods, Ready made Clothing, Boots, Shoes, Crockery and Stoneware, Groceries and Provisions in heavy Stocks. We solicit the Patronage of our Friends and hope to increase our Business by fair dealing and promt fulfilments of all engagements. P.O. Address Union Pier, Mich.
John F. Gowdy...Township Treasurer and Farmer. Sec. 25
E.O. Alliger...Post Master, Union Pier.
J.A. Wilkinson...Highway Commissioner and Farmer. Sec. 19
John S. Gibson...Proprietor of Steam Mill and Dealer in Lumber, Shingles and Cord Wood. Sec. 19.
J.H. Spaulding...Post Master and Farmer. Troy Station.
O.C. Gillette...Lumber Dealer, Brown's Station.
W.A. Keith...Supervisor and Farmer. Sec. 12.
R.C. Brewer...Practical Farmer."

Although most of the business descriptions seem rather prosaic, the list includes some of the key figures in early Chikaming history. A. (Albert) L. Drew arrived in Lakeside around 1860 and married Annis Fisher. Her photo is on page 53. R. (Richard) M. Goodwin and John F. Gowdy, along with several others, formed the partnership that built the pier and lumber operations at Union Pier. A generation later, the Gowdy family developed one of the first resort communities in Union Pier. J.A. (James Abdon) Wilkinson was the oldest son of John Wesley Wilkinson, whose mill and pier formed the nucleus of Lakeside. John S. Gibson was a steam engine mechanic, originally from New Hampshire, who managed the Wilkinson mill for a decade before starting his own lumber operation. He was also Lakeside's first postmaster.

An early farm, Mansfield's Vineyard, is shown in this photo from the late 1910s or early 1920s.

Union Pier's station was originally called Town Line, since it sat on the border between Chikaming and New Buffalo Townships. Later, the name was changed to Union Pier, name of the town's post office. This photo from the 1920s shows locals waiting at the station for weekend guests.

Early Union Pier settlers Almond Toffelmire and his wife, Ann (opposite), were married in 1881 and ran a farm, called Rattlesnake Ranch locally, along the Galien River.

This postcard, from around 1915, shows the Toffelmire Farm and Galien River.

Union Pier's business district in the 1930s included a gas station (left) and a restaurant (center).

Pictured here is John D's Cafe in Union Pier in the 1930s. A sign in front of the restaurant advertises 50-cent chicken dinners.

This 1910 photo of Dreamland shows swimmers diving from a dock and a boatload of sailors arriving.

This arch welcomed visitors to Gordon's Beach and the Gordon Beach Inn in the 1920s. The Inn became a popular resort during Union Pier's first tourist heyday.

The Lake View Hotel, shown here in the early 1920s, is another resort that has survived from Union Pier's early days of tourism.

Another Union Pier resort, the Libuse Inn, featured a double-decker screened porch.

Kucera's summer resort, pictured here around 1917, advertised that it was just 66 miles from Chicago.

Sturgeon Beach was named for the large number of sturgeon attracted to its shore. As recently as the 1950s, 200-pound specimens were caught in Lake Michigan. This photo shows a resort at Sturgeon beach in the 1930s.

Some beach accommodations, like the shack shown in this photo taken near Dreamland around 1910, were quite basic. Meals were often served in a communal dining room.

Three

LAKESIDE

By the 1840s, farmland in New Buffalo began running out, and settlers started moving to the area north of the Galien River to what is now Lakeside. An early settler, wanting to preserve the area's Indian heritage, named it Chikaming, an Algonquin word that means "at the shore of the sea."

Land was cheaper in Chikaming, and the heavily wooded area was ripe for the lumber trade. Operating under the name J.N. Wilkinson & Company, three Wilkinson brothers (John W., Joseph N., and Dr. James), recent arrivals from Virginia, built a sawmill powered by a 20-horsepower steam engine that produced 6,000 feet of lumber a day. By the 1850s, the area was known as Wilkinson, and the Wilkinson family owned 2,500 acres of lakeshore land centered on the intersection of what is now Lakeshore Road and Pier Street. The family built a 600-foot pier from which their schooner, the *Enterprise*, sailed for Chicago's big lumber markets. At Chicago, the *Enterprise* was reloaded with supplies for the family's thriving trading post on the opposite shore.

In 1874, Wilkinson was renamed Lakeside. According to one account, John W. Wilkinson's southern sympathies during the Civil War clashed with the sensibilities of local residents. Between 1860 and 1870, the population of Chikaming Township, which had been incorporated in 1856, tripled. An 1860 map shows a sawmill and a trading post, and lists 34 houses in Lakeside. In 1874, the town got a village post office, located in the Gibson home. Early Lakeside settlers John Wesley and Samantha Wilkinson were known as "Old Gentleman Wilkinson" and "Old Lady Wilkinson." In 1880, the couple donated land for the Lakeside Methodist Episcopal Church, built the following year. Children gathered berries and played ball in the lot next to the church.

FROM BOARDS TO BERRIES

As the timber was cleared, the land became used for orchards, vineyards, and berry farms. Apples, peaches, grapes, and strawberries thrived in the soil and found the climate favorable. Lakeside—indeed, much of Harbor Country—became a center of fruit and vegetable growing, and much of its crop was shipped across the lake to Chicago, by then a major city.

Lakeside residents had always appreciated the beauty of the area and expressed their pleasure in the lake with its ever-changing moods, the brilliant colors of the foliage in autumn, and the spectacular sunsets. Out-of-towners began to appreciate these features as well, and the community was on its way to becoming a resort. Some early residents lived in tents while they waited for their cottages to be built. By the late 1880s, the village began to attract tourists in earnest. A train stopped at the town, and early visitors were often faculty members and administrators from the University of Chicago. The Chikaming Country Club was established in 1910 as even more tourists flocked to the community. The Country Club's Shakespeare

House was dismantled from its home in Chicago and rebuilt piece-by-piece in Lakeside. As the town grew and Red Arrow Highway was constructed, the Wilkinson Trading Post was moved closer to the highway. This building now houses The Wilkinson Museum and some shops.

Built to accommodate the growing tourist trade, The Lakeside Inn attracted movie stars and Chicago celebrities. Legend has it that Al Capone and Chicago politicians met to drink and gamble at the Inn during Prohibition. By the early years of the 20th century, Lakeside was a famous resort. A 1910–1920 map of Lakeside lists 139 houses and their owners: tradesmen, farmers, fishermen, teachers, nurses, and the E.K. Warren family, owners of the Featherbone Factory in Three Oaks, who preferred the lakeshore to the inland town. The list notes that some of the houses were rented out for the summer to judges and professors, and house #99 was rented to Jane Addams of Hull House fame.

Tourists continue to spend their holidays here and Lakeside is also home to antique stores, restaurants, specialty shops, and inns.

Annis Fisher Drew was the daughter of Abigail and William Fisher, who moved to Lakeside c. 1850. Albert Drew, her future husband, arrived about 10 years later.

Wilkinson Lodge was Lakeside's first real home. It was built in 1863. John Wesley Wilkinson and his wife Samantha held a number of "singing evenings" in this house.

The Wilkinson house on Pier Street was built by James Abdon and Mary Annis Wilkinson. At the time this photo was taken, in the early years of the 20th century, the house was owned by their son, Clarence, and his wife, Lydia.

Another view of the Wilkinson house shows the house shaded by tall trees. The maple trees on Pier Street were planted by James Abdon Wilkinson.

LYDIA WILKINSON, LAKESIDE'S RENAISSANCE WOMAN

Harbor Country produced some remarkably energetic and talented people in its early days, and few accomplished more than Lydia Wilkinson. Lydia came to Lakeside in 1902 after marrying into one of the town's founding families. She and her husband, Clarence, had a hand in many of the events that shaped Lakeside in the first half of the 20th century. The couple ran the Pine

Bluff Hotel, a resort Clarence built the year before Lydia arrived. In 1910, the Lakeside Association leased the Pine Bluff and renamed it the Chikaming Country Club, with Clarence as manager.

Five years later, Lydia and a neighbor, Maud Perham, started Lakeside's first taxi service. They met vacationers from Chicago at the town's railroad station in their Model Ts and carted them off to the community's burgeoning resorts or private summer cottages. Clarence laid out Lakeside's golf course in 1913, and Lydia became an avid golfer.

When her husband died in 1928, Lydia took over the family real estate business and managed the Chikaming Club's clubhouses. Four years later, when the club could no longer afford a full-time manager, Lydia agreed to run the property on commission. In 1935, the post office moved to John P. Gibson's new store, and Lydia was postmistress until 1938. Three years later, she returned to manage the Country Club, but resigned the following year. The club (but not the golf course) was sold to the Sisters of the Holy Cross, who converted it and another property into a girls' summer camp called Marie du Lac.

Lydia and another neighbor, Ethel Edwards, also formed a group called Mothers and Others to support the Lakeside School. In 1947, it became the local PTA.

The Wilkinson barn on what was known as the "Point" on Pier Street and Lakeside Road. The barn was built in 1869 and was still very much in use when this photo was taken in the first decade of the 20th century. The Township Hall was later built on the site.

This photo of Clarence and Lydia Wilkinson with their daughter, Geraldine, in a wicker buggy was taken between 1901 and 1910.

On a warm afternoon around 1910, elegantly dressed ladies enjoy a backyard afternoon tea at the Wilkinson home on Pier Street. These tea parties were highlights of the day. Another resident, Mrs. O'Connor, was famous for hosting "Sunbonnet Parties," to which all girls and ladies were invited as long as they wore hats.

Dressed for a Sunday drive, Florence Robinson and a friend, identified only as Ray, pose behind a prop in a photographer's studio in St. Joseph, Michigan in August 1909.

The Jane Addams Cottage is pictured in this postcard, printed after 1907. The founder of Hull House lived next door to Eleanor Smith, head of the Hull House Music School and later a music instructor at the University of Chicago. The first membership certificate in the Chikaming Country Club—whose objectives were to provide social intercourse and promote social amusements and outdoor life and sports—was issued to Addams.

In 1913, Clarence Wilkinson and Paul Warren began pounding tin cans into the ground of Wilkinson's cornfield and laid out a golf course. This is the pond at the golf course, located east of the railroad. In 1914, The Lakeside Golf Club was organized and Harvey Collins, a pro from the Flossmoor Country Club, helped plan the links-style nine-hole course. In 1918, the golf club and Chikaming Country Club were consolidated.

Clarence Wilkinson built the Pine Bluff Hotel resort in 1901, and took this photo in August of that year. He brought his wife, Lydia Burgie, here the following year. Wilkinson's resort was on the lake, on the south side of Pier Street. In 1910, the Lakeside Association was formed and recommended the resort be leased and called Chikaming Country Club, with Clarence Wilkinson as its manager.

The Shakespeare House was a replica of Shakespeare's birthplace, and had been located next to the International Amphitheater in Chicago. It was dismantled and rebuilt in Lakeside, and became part of the Chikaming Country Club. On this postcard of the Country Club, mailed in 1928, the writer notes that he made the trip from Chicago in two hours.

This image depicts the lawn at the Lakeview Resort in the early 1900s.

The Orchard Beach Pavilion was located across the street from The Pebble House. In March of 1925, several families who were concerned about Lakeside's development bought the pavilion and had it torn down.

The Vagabond Inn on Red Arrow Highway is now Warren Woods Inn.

The Warren Pier at Lakeside, Mich.

This picture of a ruined pier dates to the early 1900s. In the second half of the 19th century, logs were brought to Lakeside, milled, and loaded onto ships tied to the pier. Once the area's lumber had been cleared, the piers were neglected and, after a few winters, they went to ruin.

In downtown Lakeside, land for the Methodist Church (left), was donated by John W. and Samantha Wilkinson. The church was built in 1881.

In this picture, people wait for the train at Wilkinson Station in Lakeside around 1910. When school was out, the women and children of summer families arrived. Each Friday night after the week's work was done, the men came from Chicago to join their families. The Pere Marquette Railroad stopped at Lakeside, and the Michigan Central stopped in nearby New Buffalo. The Friday night train was due to arrive at 7:00, though it was often delayed.

The grocery store and post office across from the depot are seen in this photo taken between 1901 and 1910. In 1900, Emery Glidden and his brothers became owners of a store on the east side of Main Street. Mr. Wilkinson was part-owner of the store. The train slowed down at Lakeside, and one mail sack was thrown from the train while another was picked up by a hook, which snagged the mail from a pair of wooden arms fastened close to the tracks.

Despite the relatively late date, this postcard of Lakeside in 1913 shows that horse-drawn carriages were still the preferred means of transportation in town.

This summertime group poses in front of the old Wilkinson Trading Post when it stood south of the church in early 1900. Nadra Kissman, great-great granddaughter of J.W. Wilkinson, and her husband, Al, bought the building and renovated it in the early 1970s. The Wilkinson Heritage Museum was founded by Nadra and her aunt, Ruth Robinson Carr, another descendant of early settlers. The museum preserves the history of Lakeside and houses a collection of photos, documents, scrapbooks, clothing, and implements.

Pictured here are the Lakeside station, general store, and post office in the early 1900s. According to the person who wrote this postcard, "the only excitement to be had is to go meet the train." When her houseguests complained of boredom, Eleanor Wilson hired a local boy from the garage to stage a mock holdup. Donning a mask and brandishing a cap gun, he ordered the surprised guests to hand over their money.

This image depicts a group of Lakeside cottages in 1922. The street to the lower right is Ashland Avenue.

Early resort areas were built in the southern part of Lakeside. Much of this area was developed as a resort which came to be known as Orchard Beach Cottages.

This view of Pier Street Beach dates to 1901. Pilings from the old pier are visible in the background.

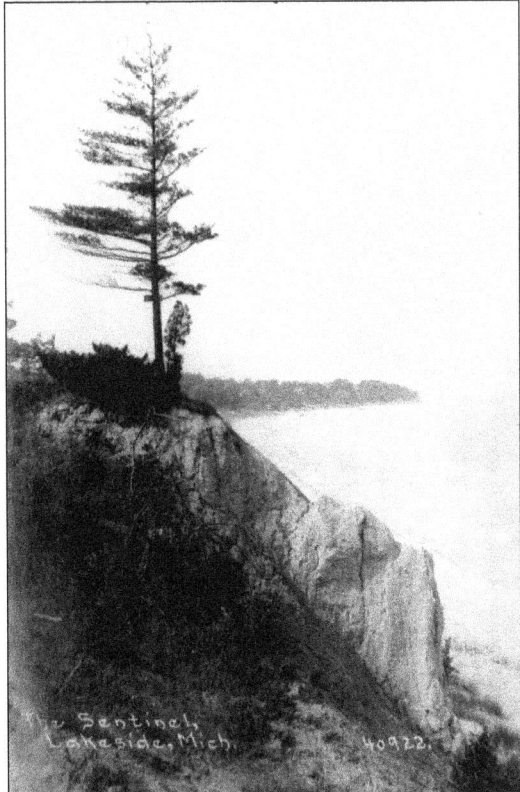

Pictured here is the Sentinel, a landmark on the shores of Lake Michigan in Lakeside.

"We are enjoying this lovely place and the children are growing brown and rugged," wrote a summer visitor to Lakeside on this 1909 postcard. For Chicagoans, the beaches provided relaxation and exercise. The surrounding woods were cool and full of wildflowers.

This was a section of Lakeside's shoreline in 1926.

On Way to the Beach,
Lakeside, Mich.   40942-c

A set of beach stairs, photographed around 1925, descends a bluff on Lakeside's shoreline.

THE RAVINE AT PINE BLUFF
LAKESIDE, MICH.

The Ravine at Pine Bluff is pictured c. 1911.

View of M 11, Lakeside, Mich. 39907-nr

This is a view of Highway M-11 (Lakeshore Rd.) in the late 1920s. Work on M-11, one of Harbor Country's earliest roads, began in the 1830s. The highway followed an old Indian trail.

Four

THREE OAKS

Although the farms and sawmills of early settlers dotted the area around Three Oaks by the 1830s, the village's origins go back to 1849, when the Michigan Central Railroad completed a section of track from Niles to New Buffalo. The railroad built sidings every few miles along its main line so that trains could load cordwood for fuel, and larger timbers for construction down the line.

Henry Chamberlain, son of an early New Buffalo settler, owned a large piece of property along one of the sidings. In 1850, he contracted with the Michigan Central to supply 4,000 cords of hardwood to fuel the ships at New Buffalo. Chamberlain began clearing the land around the siding, then known as Chamberlain's Siding, and built the future town's first house, a log cabin. Though he was just 26 years old in 1850, Chamberlain had already served twice as New Buffalo Township supervisor (and would serve a third time in 1851) and, for two years, had been a member of the Michigan State Legislature.

Chamberlain believed the area around his siding had great potential as a trading center, and in the early 1850s, he built roads through the surrounding woodlands along section lines. In 1854, he and a partner, Joseph G. Ames, built a store and a house on one of the roads, now called Elm Street. Shortly afterward, a warehouse and more houses—probably occupied by lumbermen—went up, and a log schoolhouse was built on the corner of Ash and Elm.

In 1856, Three Oaks and Chikaming Townships split off from New Buffalo Township, and the following year the town was platted and the railroad began making regular stops. A decade later, in 1867, the Village of Three Oaks was incorporated. The village took its name from a group of three large oak trees, a landmark for railroad passengers and crews, near the siding.

By the 1870s, several manufacturers had set up shop in Three Oaks. One made barrel heads and staves. Another made wooden pipes: logs were bored lengthwise, bound with iron and treated with creosote, then used to carry water.

THE FEATHERBONE FACTORY COMES TO TOWN

What really put Three Oaks on the map, however, was a material called featherbone, patented in 1883 by Edward K. Warren, a local shopkeeper. Warren, and a partner from Michigan City named George Holden, figured out a way to make a light, stiff tape from shredded turkey feather quills. Featherbone turned out to be a big improvement over whalebone, used at the time to stiffen women's corsets and other garments. The new material didn't turn brittle with age, it was easier for garment-makers to use, and it came at a time when whaling was in decline.

In its first year, the Warren Featherbone Company managed just $7,000 in sales, but by the end of the second, sales had increased more than tenfold, and in 1886, they rose to $200,000. Warren and Holden opened additional plants in Michigan, Indiana and Canada, and sales offices in major U.S. and foreign cities. In 1885, Warren began manufacturing buggy whips made of featherbone,

HOW TO MAKE FEATHERBONE

When Edward Warren and George Holden patented featherbone in 1883, their invention made headlines in the trade press. One article described the process thus:

"The first thing is to strip the feathers of their plumage. Rollers with knives attached split the quills in half. Sandpaper rollers revolving rapidly remove the pith. Then, a series of interlocking knives reduce the quills to fiber. In this state, the material is fed into a machine that forms it into a strong, fine cord, at the same time it is being wound with thread. In another machine, four of these tightly wound cords are wound together with thread, in such a manner as to form a flat tape."

Unlike whalebone, featherbone could be produced in long sections, which made it easier for garment manufacturers to use. Featherbone also didn't turn brittle, as whalebone often did. For nearly half a century, until plastics replaced it, featherbone was the material of choice for stays and corsets, and it made Warren, who died in Evanston, Illinois in 1919, a very wealthy man.

and Three Oaks attracted a factory for their production. The effect of the two industries was to double the town's population in the late 1880s to about 1,500, not much less than it is currently.

Corsets and buggy whips are classic examples of product obsolescence, and by the first decades of the 20th century, demand for featherbone began to dwindle. Warren's factory stayed alive, thanks to some diversification and a modest resurgence in demand for fashions that required stays. In 1938, the company still employed between 300 and 400 people. The Warren Featherbone Company, incidentally, is still in business, though today it makes clothing for newborns and infants. Its headquarters moved from Three Oaks to Gainesville, Georgia in 1955.

EDWARD K. WARREN'S LEGACY

Warren's invention made him wealthy, and perhaps his upbringing—he was the son of a Congregational minister who moved to Three Oaks from Vermont in 1858—made him philanthropic. During the Featherbone Company's heyday, it donated $250 annually to the town on the condition that saloons be kept out. In 1904, Warren was elected president of the World Sunday School, and he built guest houses in Lakeside for visiting missionaries.

But Warren's most lasting contribution, two years before his death in 1919, was the donation of 300 acres of old-growth forest between Three Oaks and Lakeside, and of another 289 acres of dunes along Lake Michigan north of Sawyer. The former became Warren Woods State Park; the latter Warren Dunes State Park.

Three Oaks made headlines in 1899 when President William McKinley came to town to present the village with a cannon captured by Admiral George Dewey in Manila the previous year. Answering a call for donations for a memorial to servicemen who died when the *Maine* sank in Havana's harbor, Three Oaks' citizens pledged more per capita than any other town in America: $1.41. The cannon was placed—and remains—in a park built specially for it across from the old railroad station.

Today, Three Oaks is best known for its annual Flag Day Parade—the world's largest, say its promoters—and the Apple Cider Century, an annual bicycle tour started in 1974 that every fall draws thousands of cyclists to the village and the country roads around it. The town also starred in a 1989 movie, *Prancer*, and in a sequel filmed 12 years later.

Thanks mostly to decades of relative somnolence, Three Oaks has preserved much of its early architecture and a small-town ambience that a growing number of weekenders and second-home owners prefer to the more crowded, faster-paced harbor and restaurants of New Buffalo.

Originally named Chamberlain's Siding after an early settler, Three Oaks acquired its current name in 1854. It was named for a clump of three oak trees that grew near the train tracks. The trees were used as a landmark by railroad workers. The original oaks were described as "massive." The three trees shown in this early 20th century postcard of Dewey Cannon Park are probably not the originals.

This bird's-eye view looks northeast along North Elm Street. When this postcard was mailed in 1908, Three Oaks' commercial district was already well-established. Among the businesses pictured are a livery stable and a farm implements store.

A lone horse-drawn carriage makes its way northbound on Elm Street. A livery stable is in the foreground and a Warren Featherbone Co. building is on the right in the background. A sign on one of the telephone poles advertises a state fair.

This is an image of North Elm Street, looking north, from a 1907 postcard. The structure on left is the E.K. Warren Building, now the library.

Birds-eye View South, Three Oaks, Mich. 54031-r

This overhead view of Three Oaks looks south on Elm Street near the railroad tracks. The street is shared by a bicycle, horses, and an automobile.

The Warren Featherbone Co. was a big business in the early 1900s when this photo of its factories was taken. In a 1938 history of Three Oaks, the author notes that in that year, the company still had between 300 and 400 employees on its payroll, thanks mostly to a resurgence in fashions that required stays, and diversification into other millinery items. Many of the factory buildings are still standing, and are occupied by newer businesses.

View of Chas. K. Warren & Co's Store, Three Oaks, Mich. 54026-R

The Chas. K. Warren & Co. general store is pictured in the early 20th century. The first commercial building in Three Oaks was a general store owned by Henry Chamberlain and Joseph Ames in 1854.

76

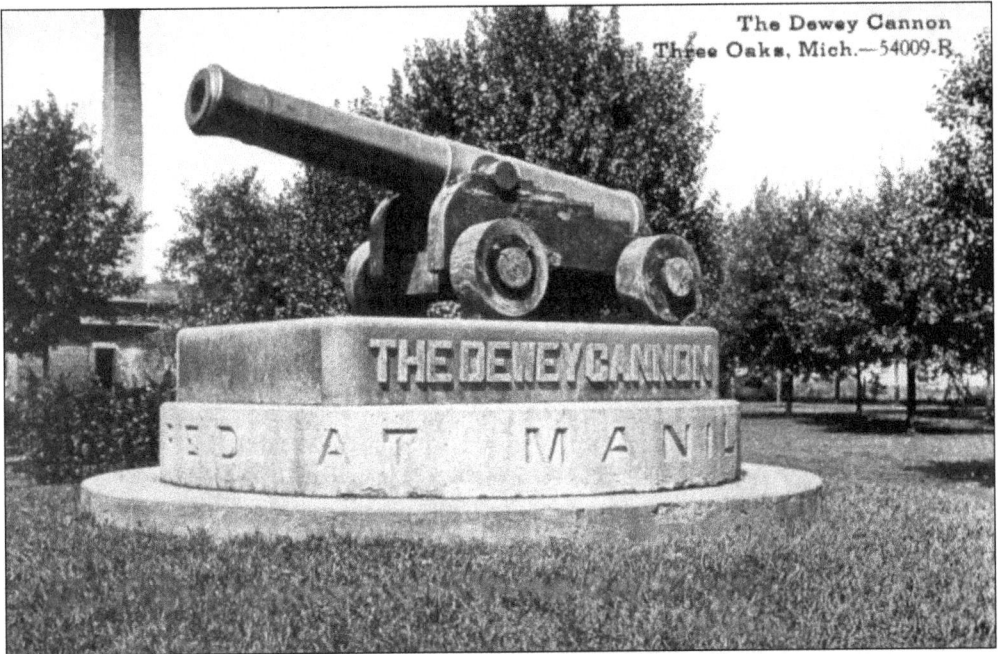

Citizens of Three Oaks raised $1,400 to help pay for a memorial to the crew of the battleship *Maine* in 1898, during the Spanish-American War. The contribution was the largest, per capita, of any community in the country, and the town was honored with a visit from President William McKinley in 1899. A year later, Three Oaks was presented with a cannon captured by Admiral George Dewey in Manila. The so-called Dewey Cannon still sits in a park, which was named for it, behind the Three Oaks railroad station.

Though the Featherbone Company dominated Three Oaks' economy in the early part of the 20th century, it was not the only business in town, as this postcard of a cannery, postmarked 1919, shows.

This dairy, another local business, served Three Oaks in the early 1900s.

As Three Oaks thrived in the late 19th and early 20th century, new housing was built to accommodate the village's growing population. In this photo, the streets are electrically lit, but still unpaved, and the streetside trees are still saplings.

In this photo of South Elm Street, taken around 1912, the trees are more mature, though the street is still unpaved. The village's old Victorian houses give Three Oaks much of its current charm.

The town installed its first municipal water system in 1896. This water tower was part of that system when this postcard was mailed in 1909.

This is the Michigan Central Railroad station in Three Oaks, as it appeared around 1912. Passenger trains no longer stop in Three Oaks, and the station, little changed since it was built in 1898, is now the Three Oaks Bicycle Museum and Information Center.

Three Oaks built its first public school, a log building, in 1854. It was replaced by a frame structure three years later. The brick schoolhouse in this 1918 photo was built in 1877 and expanded and remodeled in 1896.

Three Oaks' Congregational Church, shown here around 1920, was originally organized in New Buffalo in 1844. The Congregational Church, finished in 1870, was the first church building in Three Oaks.

Methodists first held services in the Three Oaks area at the home of Whitman Goit in 1833, and built their first church in town in 1878. The building was extensively remodeled in 1908, a few years before this photo was taken.

Pictured here are St. Mary's Church and rectory in the first decade of the 1900s. The church was built in 1880.

This image depicts the Church of Christ, Three Oaks.

Two years before his death in 1919, Edward K. Warren and his wife established the Edward K. Warren Foundation. Two of Harbor Country's gems, Warren Dunes, just north of Sawyer, and Warren Woods, between Three Oaks and Lakeside, were early gifts of the foundation. Warren Woods, pictured above, consists of 300 acres of virgin woodland along the Galien River.

The Three Oaks Spokes bicycle club sponsors the annual Apple Cider Century, a tour of Harbor Country's lakeshore and back roads that draws 6,000 cyclists for rides of between 25 and 100 miles.

The Three Oaks Bicycle Museum occupies the former Michigan Central station in the village's downtown. Exhibits include antique two-wheelers and a replica of the station's telegraph room.

Five
HARBERT

Although the town was named for a Chicago industrialist who was instrumental in building its train station, it was John Glavin, an engineer who worked on the Lake Shore and Michigan Southern Railroad, who saw the area's potential for farmland as he traveled on his runs between Chicago and Detroit. Glavin wanted to raise crops on the barren land, and the price was affordable. Switching careers, he farmed the land and founded the community in 1850. Glavin's hunch was right, and the area's soil and climate proved perfect for growing for grapes and other fruit. Greenbush Pier was located two miles west of Sawyer and one mile north of Harbert. Greenbush was the name given to a swampy area that remained green almost year round. Both the pier and the sawmill town near it were called Greenbush before they were renamed Harbert when a railroad depot was established there.

Since then, Harbert has been an agricultural community with orchards and vineyards. The town's agricultural bounty found its way to the depot, and from there the produce was shipped to either Chicago or Detroit. Pulitzer Prize-winner Carl Sandburg wrote much of his biography of Abraham Lincoln while he lived at his Harbert home. He became the community's most famous visitor, and his family resided in Harbert for 15 years. Sandburg loved the peace and tranquility of the area's dunes, beaches, and woods. Sandburg also raised prize goats, which he shipped across the country to goat breeders. Today, Harbert's fields are dotted with antique stores and family restaurants.

Pictured here is the Harbert Depot. The railroad was instrumental in the growth of the town, since local produce was shipped from here to Chicago and Detroit. Later, the train brought summer vacationers.

View of the Apple Grove Service Station as seen from M-11 in Harbert, Michigan. The business was established by the Tournquists, and was later owned by their daughter, Maxine Patejdl.

This is a view of Hibbs Pond in Harbert *c.* 1907.

This image depicts "Wray" the fisherman, mending his nets in 1907. Though sport fishing is still popular around Harbor Country, commercial fishing no longer contributes to the area's economy.

These are the beach stairs leading to Point Comfort on Lake Michigan in the early 20th century.

The back of this 1913 postcard advertises one of Harbert's resorts. It reads: "Birchwood Beach Near to Nature's heart at Harbert on M-11, Three hours from Chicago. Birchwood offers you good pure food, water, air, sunshine, and economy."

Pictured here is Catalpa Road, Prairie Club, in Harbert.

This is Bonny Castle at Birchwood Beach.

Sandburg's Goats are pictured at Flat Rock, North Carolina. During his 15-year stay in Harbert, Sandburg raised prize-winning goats and wrote much of his biography of Abraham Lincoln. This image is from the Sandburgs' 1946 Christmas card.

A postcard from the 1930s calls this place at Birchwood Beach, "Lovers' Paradise." A guest wrote, "When we find a couple of boy friends we're going to take them here."

Six

SAWYER

Sawyer marks the northernmost limit of Harbor Country. The community got off the ground when Silas Sawyer, an Ohio judge, came to the area in 1853. The land was originally covered by a maple-beech forest, marshes, hardwood swamps, and evergreen swamps. Oak and walnut trees reached 15 feet in circumference.

Judge Sawyer bought 100 acres of land, cleared half of it and planted that with fruit trees. He continued to log the other half of his land, hauling the timber on a horse-driven railroad to Fuller Pier, now the site of Warren Dunes State Park. Sawyer built a steam sawmill one mile from the lake.

The community's lumber trade continued to grow, as did its orchards and farms. An open-air market was established in Sawyer so that produce could be transported to other towns via wagon or railroad. Silas Sawyer was the first supervisor of Chikaming Township in 1856. That year, 310 residents were living in the town.

John Flynn arrived in Sawyer in 1928 and built both the Palm Tea Room and the Flynn Soda Grill. He was a business agent for the Chicago Teamster's Union. The Flynn Building, which became the town's most prominent building, also housed the Flynn Theater, which staged live productions. Rumor had it that Flynn had connections with a Chicago mob.

In the 1920s, the Congregational Church built Tower Hill Camp. Warren Dunes State Park, a 1,500-acre preserve located on the Red Arrow Highway between Sawyer and Bridgman, draws over a million people a year. Michigan's most popular park, Warrren Dunes includes a two-mile stretch of white sandy beaches, camping facilities, dunes that soar to more than 240 feet, and nature trails of wildflowers and mature forest. Hang-gliding lures the adventurous to the top of the majestic dunes. Sledding and cross-country skiing are popular in winter.

Today's many happy campers can thank Edward K. Warren of Lakeside and Three Oaks, who had the foresight to buy the land that today comprises Warren Woods and the core of Warren Dunes State Park. A shrewd businessman, avid conservationist, and magnanimous philanthropist, Warren wanted to preserve the beauty of land that others considered worthless, and purchased the areas which today are natural treasures.

Continuing a tradition begun by a judge who got tired of the courtroom and city life and who turned his attention to farming and logging, Sawyer today is dotted with many vineyards, fruit orchards, and a large garden center.

Bethany Beach, founded in 1906 by a group of Swedish Baptists from the South Side of Chicago, continues to attract visitors. Begun as a faith-based summer camp, Bethany Beach is now a year-round community populated by the descendants of the original settlers. This photo, probably from the 1920s, shows the general store in the background.

This is another view of Bethany Beach from a postcard mailed in 1919. The message reads, "Just got back from lake, water was fine. Waves went very high but I think it is fun then but those that can swim like it smooth."

Pictured here is one of the cottages at Bethany Beach. There appears to be a young girl in a hammock in the left foreground of the photo.

A site known as Sulphur Springs, Bethany Beach, is pictured in this image from the mid-1920s. Mentions of mineral springs around Harbor Country appear fairly often in early accounts of the area.

In the 1940s, when this photo was taken, accommodations at Bethany Beach were spartan.

The general store at Bethany Beach supplied campers with groceries and gasoline.

This photo captures the Girls' Compound at Tower Hill Camp. Tower Hill was founded in 1922. The United Church of Christ, Illinois Conference, sponsors meetings, retreats, adult education, and sports camps at this facility, which can house 140 guests.

"Where We Eat",
Tower Hill Camp,
Sawyer, Mich.
39909-nr

This photo shows the dining hall at Tower Hill Camp.

This photo provides a view of the Sandburg Cottage from Tower Hill Beach.

This postcard shows the north group at Maple Cabins in Sawyer, and notes that they're heated. It also notes that the cabins are three quarters of a mile from the "new" Warren Dunes State Park, which dates the photo to the late 1910s or early 1920s.

Pictured here is Alexander Knaute's general store.

This photo of downtown Sawyer, taken in the early 1900s, shows the J.H. Wester Store.

This image depicts Main Street in Sawyer, with another view of the J.H. Wester Store advertising ice cream, general merchandise, flour, and feed.

This photo of Sawyer's Main Street in the 1920s or 1930s shows a gas station and store on the right, and the Flynn Building on the left.

The Palm Tea Room and Palm Soda Grill were housed in the Flynn Building, the largest building in Sawyer and home to the Flynn Theater, which staged live performances and cultural events. In 1931, the Flynn Theater was showing "all talking" movies. Vaudeville acts were performed between movies. Some say Mr. Flynn was cozy with a notorious Chicago mob, but local residents liked to think of him as an upstanding citizen who wanted to bring culture to town. During the Depression, Flynn lost his prominence in the Teamster's Union and the Flynn Theater closed its doors. Through the years it has served as a machine shop, warehouse, auction barn, and archery range.

The Tune Inn on U.S. 12 in Sawyer advertised "wonderfully good food" as well as its location midway between Michigan City and St. Joseph.

Seven

GRAND BEACH

By the first years of the 20th century, the southern part of New Buffalo Township along the lakefront had been stripped of much of its original pine forest—the lumber used for telegraph poles and railroad ties. Oaks were growing where the pine had once stood, and a few acres had been cleared for farming by early settlers Michael Bock and August Vetterly. Much of the area, then known as Wildwood Park, was government-owned, thanks in part to tax seizures.

Sometime around 1903, an executive with the Fuller Advertising Company in Chicago, Floyd R. Perkins, began buying up parcels along the shore and built a hunting shack near Forest Beach. Perkins' plan was to turn the land into a hunting preserve, but after a few years of unsuccessful effort, he abandoned that plan and decided to put the property up for sale. He hired a copywriter to put together an ad for his Michigan real estate and liked what he read so much that he decided to keep it and develop it as a resort. He persuaded another Chicago ad man, George H. Ely of Stark Promotions, to join him in a partnership called the Grand Beach Company.

Together, Perkins and Ely bought more land, often at a bargain in tax sales. Eventually, they put together a 700-acre tract, including a four-mile stretch of beach. The company hired Phillip Hesse as manager and agent for the new resort, which it called Grand Beach Springs for several natural springs on the property. Later, it changed the name to Grand Beach Park, and finally, just Grand Beach.

SUMMER COTTAGES BY SEARS

With Hesse in charge, work began in earnest. Around 1907, he built three cottages: one for his family, one for use as a dining hall for workers, and a third for an office. That same year, he ordered 20 one-room cottages from Sears and set them up near the lakeshore as rental units. A bit later, Hesse built another dozen two-room bungalows, which he offered for sale as summer homes. They sold quickly.

The Michigan Central Railroad had operated train service to Chicago since the 1850s, and stopped at a point called Vetterly's, not far from the entrance to Grand Beach. In 1911, the Grand Beach Company built a small station and soon, the train from Chicago stopped three times a day in Grand Beach. The trip from Chicago took 90 minutes, compared with a travel time of over three hours by car. The railroad rebuilt the station in 1912–1913, and operated it for decades. It was finally razed in 1940, after better highways made the trip from Chicago by car more practical.

In 1910, Hesse built a pair of posts to mark the entry to Grand Beach. About five years later, the local property owners' association constructed an arch atop the posts and a fence that ran alongside the tracks and Grand Beach Road. Ever since, the arch has served as the village's symbol, used on everything from its website to shirts sold in its golf shop.

GOLF AT GRAND BEACH

When Grand Beach built its first nine-hole golf course in 1911, the game's popularity was growing rapidly, and the course proved a significant draw for the resort's owners. A 1915 New York Times article, cited in Michigan Golfer, noted that the number of golfers in the U.S. had grown from 5,000 to somewhere between 2.5 and 3.5 million within the previous 10 years. By 1910, there were 23 courses in Michigan; another forty were built in the following decade.

Tom Bendelow, designer of the Grand Beach course, was the leading golf course architect of the day. He arrived in the U.S. from Scotland in 1895, just 10 years after the first golf club in the country opened in Fairfield, Connecticut. By the end of the 1920s, he had designed more than 400 courses coast to coast. Perhaps the most famous Bendelow course—though it's been much modified since he designed it as a ladies' course in 1928—is Medinah #3 outside Chicago. That course has been the site of three U.S. Opens, three Western Opens, and the 1999 PGA Championship.

In 1911, a Bendelow course had the same sort of appeal that a Pete Dye or Robert Trent Jones design has today, and the Grand Beach Company promoted the course and its famous architect shamelessly. "Any one of the [nine] holes compares favorably with any course in the country," a 1911 brochure announced. A later brochure proclaimed the course, by then expanded to 18 holes, as the equal of St. Andrew's.

At one time, Grand Beach offered 27 holes, but in the late 1930s, after the Golfmore Hotel burned, the owner of the hotel (and the golf course) sold the front nine— substantially the original Bendelow course—as well as the clubhouse and maintenance equipment to the Property Owners' Association for $6,000. He offered the back nine for another $2,000, but the group couldn't afford it and holes 10 to 18 were dropped. A few years later, when taxes on the course proved burdensome, the association donated it to the village, which continues to operate it today as a municipal course.

By the beginning of the century's second decade, Grand Beach was a popular destination, and the company made many improvements to accommodate the growing crowds. Hesse's one-room dining hall and office were joined and expanded several times over the years. By 1915, the building could accommodate 250 diners.

In 1911, the Grand Beach Company built its original nine-hole golf course, designed by Tom Bendelow, the premier course architect of the day. That same year, the company erected a clubhouse at the corner of Royal and Crescent near the site of a sulfur spring. Variously known as the Golf Inn and the Men's Club, the clubhouse offered showers and lockers and overnight accommodations for visiting golfers. By 1917, the course had expanded to 18 holes (the back nine were north of the present course), and by the 1920s, the 18 had been expanded to 27.

As the number of summer visitors grew, a 21-room inn, The Lodge, was built on the corner of Lakeview and Royal. A short time later, another inn, the Pinewood Inn (also known at various times at the Pinewood Lodge, Midwestwood, Midwest Pine Inn and Hayes Inn) went up on Station Road. After World War I, Grand Beach experienced a building boom, as more Chicagoans built lavish summer houses on the lake. Frank Lloyd Wright designed three of them.

THE GOLFMORE HOTEL

Grand Beach was already firmly on the tourist map when its crowning touch, the Golfmore Hotel, opened for business in 1921. A massive, 175-room resort hotel with room for 500 guests, the Golfmore offered—in addition to golf—horseback riding, tennis, rental boats and even a ski jump for winter visitors. Its guests included movie stars and other celebrities.

Perkins and Ely disagreed over the wisdom of building the hotel, and Ely withdrew from the partnership. His decision, it turned out, was prescient. By 1927, the Grand Beach Company, which then owned the hotel and golf course, went into bankruptcy. After passing in and out of receivership, the hotel was acquired by Albert E. Berger in 1936. Berger planned to turn it into a casino. There was opposition to his plan, but the question was finally settled for good three years later, when the Golfmore burned to the ground.

Beginning in the 1920s, the privately owned parts of Grand Beach were governed by a property owners' association, and maintenance and improvements were funded by voluntary donations. Since those proved unreliable, association leaders incorporated Grand Beach as a village in 1934.

Today, Grand Beach has an official population of just 146, but on any given summer weekend second-home owners and their guests bring the total to several times that. Many of those visitors are families who've been returning to Grand Beach for generations. Others have built houses on the few remaining parcels of land, and are beginning family traditions of their own.

GRAND CENTRAL STATION, GRAND BEACH, MICH.

The Grand Beach Company built the town's first Michigan Central Railroad station in 1911. It replaced an earlier stop, called Vetterly's, which served a farm once located on Grand Beach property. Phillip Hesse, Grand Beach Co. manager and agent, was also the railroad's first agent at the station.

In 1912–1913, the Michigan Central built a larger station at Grand Beach. Train service from Chicago was discontinued in the 1930s, and the railroad, unwilling to pay taxes on an unused building, tore the station down around 1940.

106

A Michigan Central Railroad ticket from Chicago to Grand Beach, dated 1920. The trip to Grand Beach took 90 minutes (compared to three hours or more by car in pre-Interstate days), and the railroad ran three trips a day in both directions. Occasionally, the railroad also ran special private cars to Grand Beach.

United States Railroad Administration
MICHIGAN CENTRAL RAILROAD
GRAND BEACH

To
Via

18761

Good for One Continuous Passage commencing not later than one day after date of sale. Subject to tariff regulations.

HALF TICKET

Form B

Gen'l Passenger Agent

CHECK to be taken up by FIRST CONDUCTOR
GRAND BEACH

18761

HALF FARE
Not Good for Passage

Form B   MICHIGAN CENTRAL RAILROAD

Beginning in 1910, Grand Beach guests were greeted at the station and taken to the office by a horse-drawn bus, shown in this undated postcard. (The bus is also visible in the photo of the train station on the opposite page.)

These posts, which later formed the base of an arch, were built in 1910 to mark the entrance to Grand Beach.

Between 1915 and 1917, the Grand Beach Property Owners' Association added the archway and fence to the 1910 posts. The arch has become the village's trademark, and its current appearance differs little from this 1920 photo.

The dining room was built in 1907 for Grand Beach Co. workers, and a one-room Sears cottage next door served as an office. The two buildings were joined and enlarged two years later, and remodeled several times again during the early part of the century. A 1915 brochure mentions the building could accommodate 250 diners. The building was razed in the winter of 1959–1960 as the Rohde Center (today's village hall and pro shop) neared completion.

Phillip Hesse built the Grand Beach Company's first houses—a group of four, including his own—at the corner of Royal and Perkins. One of the houses served as the area's first post office.

The Lodge, a 21-room inn on the corner of Royal and Lakeview, was erected in 1912. From 1935 to 1941, it was a private home, but it reopened as an inn again in 1941 and remained in operation until 1967, when it was razed. The concrete bollards lining the road were installed in 1926.

This is another view of The Lodge (left), looking east on Royal Avenue. The postcard is dated 1916. The pipes running through the bollards on the right side of the street were originally meant to carry water, but were never used for that purpose.

In 1911, Grand Beach commissioned popular golf course designer Tom Bendelow to design a nine-hole course. The Golf Inn, also known as the Men's Club and built the same year, served as a clubhouse and offered overnight accommodations to visiting golfers. In 1912, a bowling alley was added. Ironically (since the Inn was rarely open to women), the flagpole in front of the building came from the Women's Pavilion of the Columbian Exposition in Chicago. The Golf Inn was torn down in 1941, and the site became a park. In the town's earliest days, there was a sulphur spring on the property.

This photo shows the original Grand Beach Pier, built of wood in 1909 and destroyed by ice the following winter. A second pier was built in 1912, and it, too, was destroyed by lake storms in 1929. Today's pier was completed around 1973.

"A Grand Beach Home", Grand Beach, Mich.   10-gbmr

The first Grand Beach homes were modest cottages, but as the area attracted more second-home owners, some built large, costly residences, such as this 1916 house by Frank Lloyd Wright, one of three Wright houses in the village.

Through the Dunes
of Grand Beach

APPROACHING THE JUMBO DUNE

Early visitors to Grand Beach often got lost as they wandered through the dunes, then largely wooded and undeveloped. To help hikers find their way, in the early 1900s the Grand Beach Company strung ropes through the trees and brush to mark a trail. A trail map from that era (cover shown here) claims the walk "excels in natural splendor all others, and which in point of wonder equals the Grand Canyon, Yellowstone Park and the Niagara Falls."

The Pinewood Inn (also known as the Pinewood Lodge, Midwestwood, Midwest Pine Inn, and Hayes Inn) was built sometime before 1914 as the summer headquarters of the Mid West Box Company, and was used as a convention center and retreat for Chicago advertising executives. For a brief period, the inn was home to Erican, a seasonal confectionery business run by a local real estate developer. The building is now the Tall Oaks Inn.

The first Grand Beach pump house was built in 1910–1911. Several others followed until the village tied into Michiana's water supply. Pictured, from left to right, are the following: Adolph Riech, Joe Everts, Phil Hesse, and Joe Plummer.

Grand Beach, Michigan

This is an image of Grand Beach from a postcard postmarked 1912.

This is a view similar to the previous picture and taken several years later. The building in the background is probably the dining hall.

Pictured here is yet another view of the beach. By the time this postcard was made, a number of private houses lined the bluff above the shore.

Completed in 1921, the Golfmore Hotel was a 175-room luxury hotel that offered horseback riding, tennis, rental boats, and a ski jump, in addition to 27 holes of golf. When the Grand Beach Co. went bankrupt in 1927, the hotel went in and out of receivership, and finally burned to the ground in a spectacular fire in November 1939.

This is a view from the roof of the Hotel Golfmore. The foot bridge crosses White Creek (earlier known as State Creek, and the site of a sawmill). The building to the left of the bridge on the far side of the creek is the dining room, and the pier extends behind it.

The Golfmore's lakeside promenade and terraces are shown on an early postcard.

Scene at Hotel Golfmore. Grand Beach, Mich.

Shuffleboard was just one of many activities offered by the Golfmore. In 1927, a single room with shared bath cost $7 a night. Three-room suites with lake views started at $40.

Pictured here is the restaurant staff of the Golfmore Hotel, in a photo taken in 1934.

This image depicts the Lounge at the Hotel Golfmore.

Boating in Lake Michigan carries some risks, as this 1913 postcard of a wrecked sailboat being pulled ashore in Grand Beach attests.

PRIORITY OF COURSE

Players starting from any tee other than the first have no rights of priority on the course.

Players, for the protection of those following, must assert their rights under these priority rules.

Matches of three balls or more must always keep aside and allow properly constituted match —two-some, three-some, or four-some laying two balls—to pass. A properly constituted match allowing a four-ball match or three-ball match not availing themselves of this privilege, and keeping back another properly constituted match, must let the latter go through.

OUT OF BOUNDS
ALL FENCES ON COURSE

Hole 7. Hedge surrounding Channell residence.

LOST BALL

Players looking for a lost ball should allow other players coming up to pass them.

A ball lying within a club length of any direction post, tee, tee box, seat or drain cover, be dropped as near as possible to where it lies, but not nearer hole without penalty.

Ball stopping in gopher holes can be lifted and played without a penalty stroke. Players should smooth footprints in bunkers. Please replace the turf and save your course.

PROTECT THE COURSE

As a ball must be played where it lies in a trap or bunker, regardless of winter rules, players are expected to smooth over irregularities made by club or foot before leaving and not thus penalize players who follow.

Observe Golf Etiquette. Please Let Faster Players Through.

GRAND BEACH LINKS

SCORE CARD

Grand Beach, Michigan

BILL HALL, Pro

This is a 1938 scorecard from the Grand Beach golf course. Note that the card carries a drawing of the Golfmore, which also owned the course. At the time, there were 27 holes in Grand Beach. The year after this scorecard was issued, the Golfmore burned down, and its owner sold the front nine to the town's property owners' association for $6,000. In 1940, a single round of golf (9 holes) cost 50¢, and an all-day pass was $1.00.

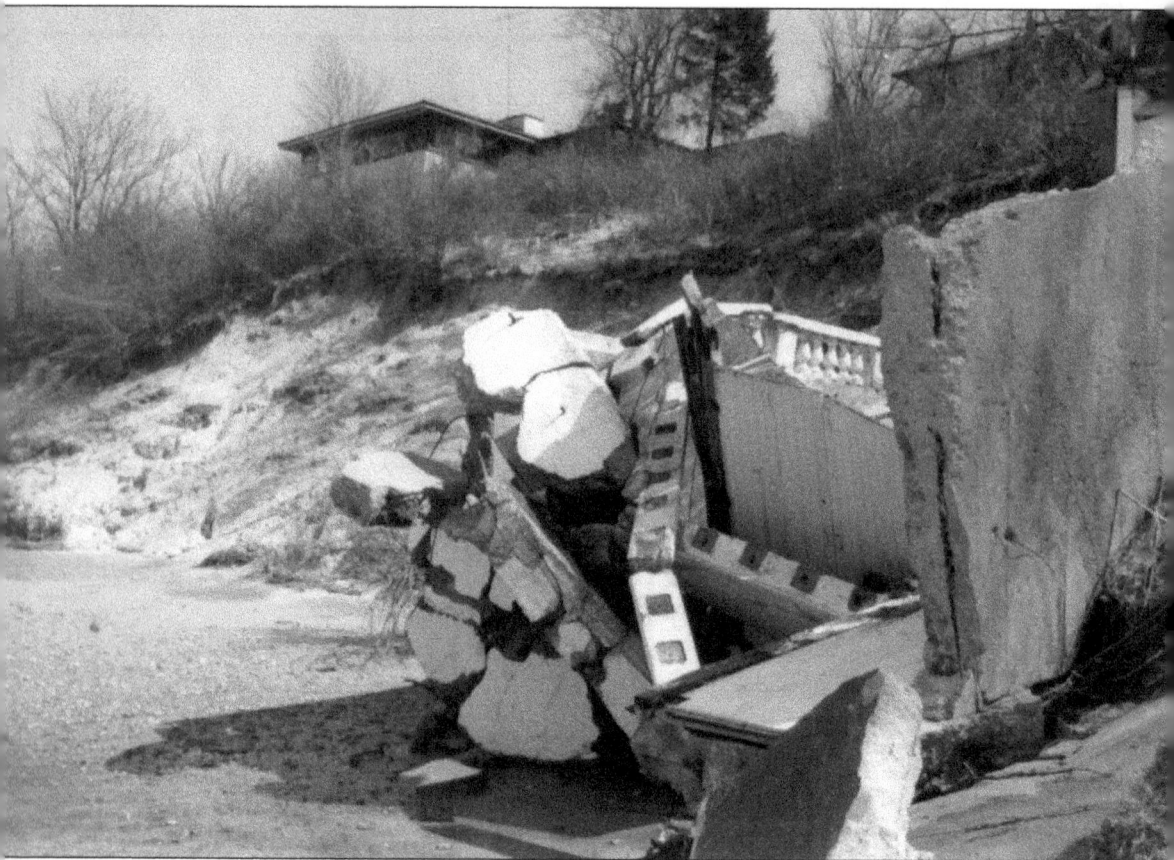

Lake storms can devastate beaches and even pull down waterfront houses. This photo, taken after a 1950 storm, shows a collapsed terrace in Grand Beach.

Eight

MICHIANA

The newest and southernmost village of Harbor Country, the Village of Michiana has always been a quiet resort community and a haven for Chicago families. The growth of The Michigan Central Railroad, the construction of the Red Arrow Highway, and a booming Chicago economy contributed to the growth of the area as more affluent Chicagoans sought peace and tranquility along the shores and dunes where they could build summer cottages. The Roaring Twenties was a time of prosperity and land speculation in the area.

Orphie Gotto, president, and Clarence Mathias, partner, formed The Long Beach Development Company. Through a series of transactions, the two bought parcels of land in what is now Michiana, and in neighboring sites. Axel Lonnquist bought part of the 600-acre parcel of what is now Michiana, Michigan, and Michiana Shores, Indiana, but had to sell it back to the Long Beach Company in 1932 due to financial difficulties. The Long Beach Company promoted the area and advertised lots with summer cottages for as little as $1,000. Although Chicagoans were being courted by the various developers who were building resort communities, these other communities prohibited the sale of land to minorities. According to a history published in honor of Michiana's 50th Anniversary, Michiana was the only town in the area where Jews could buy land. (The Grand Beach Homeowners Association, for example, suggested strongly that cottage owners rent only to Gentile families).

The Signal Tree, located at Ponchartrain Drive and Stop 37, bore the marks of the surveyors who had established the boundary between Michigan and Indiana. It was at the Signal Tree that the Long Beach Company wooed prospective buyers. As part of its campaign, the Long Beach Company built an amphitheater around the tree and held powwows and other mock-Indian ceremonies to attract and entertain would-be buyers. This site also became the meeting place for Michiana citizens, who continued to call their meetings "powwows" and decided to create a governing body in the mid 1930s. Thus the Michiana Community Association was born, and members were given a diamond-shaped metal emblem to display. A few of these emblems can still be seen today, nailed to trees in front of Michiana houses. Most of these homes, built during the 1920s and 1930s, were meant to be summer cottages. Some bore the names of their owner's profession, such as Teacher's Row and Laundry Row. Before houses in Michiana had numbers, they had names like Five Leaves, Four Roses, Gestopia and Arbutus Hill. During the 1930s and 1940s, Bill Jasch began building homes that today are considered the distinctive Michiana cottage, and over 60 of these are still standing. In an effort to duplicate the charm of the chalets of Jasch's native Switzerland, the major hallmark of a Jasch house is its smooth finished log exterior (traditionally painted brown), tall pointed roofs, low eaves, and massive stone chimneys. Jasch log homes were built on a foundation of Michigan fieldstone. Modern construction may use a foundation, but even contemporary houses still strive for the log-cabin effect. Today these and other kinds of cottages in Michiana are hidden on shady lanes and are surrounded by tall mature trees.

Zoning and Infrastructure Issues Lead to Incorporation

By the end of World War II, building codes became a concern for the village, along with other problems such as an unreliable water system and unpaved roads. It was a given that the water system refused to work at least once every day. Some residents resorted to having the roads in front of their houses oiled in an effort to reduce dust, but this proved to be a bad solution since the oil was tracked into the cottages.

The village was incorporated in the state of Michigan in 1946. Incorporation allowed the village to receive federal and state funding for roads and for improving its water system.

The Community Association could also enact and enforce building codes, since some of the residents had been unhappy with the quality of construction undertaken in previous years before the codes were enacted. Michiana now had a town council, and the Association continued to manage beach maintenance and lifeguards, and it was responsible for relocating a dangerous railroad crossing. The association remained active until 1961. Wanting to keep its simple charm, and true to its beginnings as a resort community, Michiana prohibited all industry and business, choosing to remain strictly a residential community, aware that every convenience is available a short drive away in southwest Michigan or northwest Indiana. Like its neighboring resort communities, Michiana was a place for mothers and their children to spend the summer, with the breadwinner joining the family on weekends. Since more women have joined the workforce, Michiana has become a community of weekend and year-round residents. The Community House and the tennis courts provide a meeting place for Michiana dwellers, who continue to believe that their town is the best place in the world to live and hope that this love will continue for its generations to come.

This photo of the Rosenberg cottage on Pontchartrain in Michiana was taken in 1936, the year the house was built and shortly after the area was developed by the Long Beach Company. In the early 1930s, a lot with a cottage could be had for as little as $1,000.

Pictured on the steps of
their Michiana cottage
are, from left to right,
Minnie Baldauf, Harry O. Rosenberg,
Helena B. Rosenberg,
Harry B. Rosenberg, and
Gertrude Flexner Baldauf. This
photo was taken in 1936 or 1937.

Harry B. Rosenberg posed for this photo
on a hill between Stops 40 and 41 in
Michiana in September 1936.

This wintry photo of a frozen Lake Michigan was taken from the stairs at Stop 41. Buses out of nearby Michigan City used to arrive every half hour in Michiana. The buses stopped at every intersection along the town's Lake Shore Drive. Every bus stop in Michiana from Stop 37 to Stop 42 is still called a stop, even though the buses ceased running long ago, and each stop features a shelter such as this.

Sally Rosenberg Romansky and babysitter Jean Frye are pictured on the beach in Michiana in the mid-1960s.

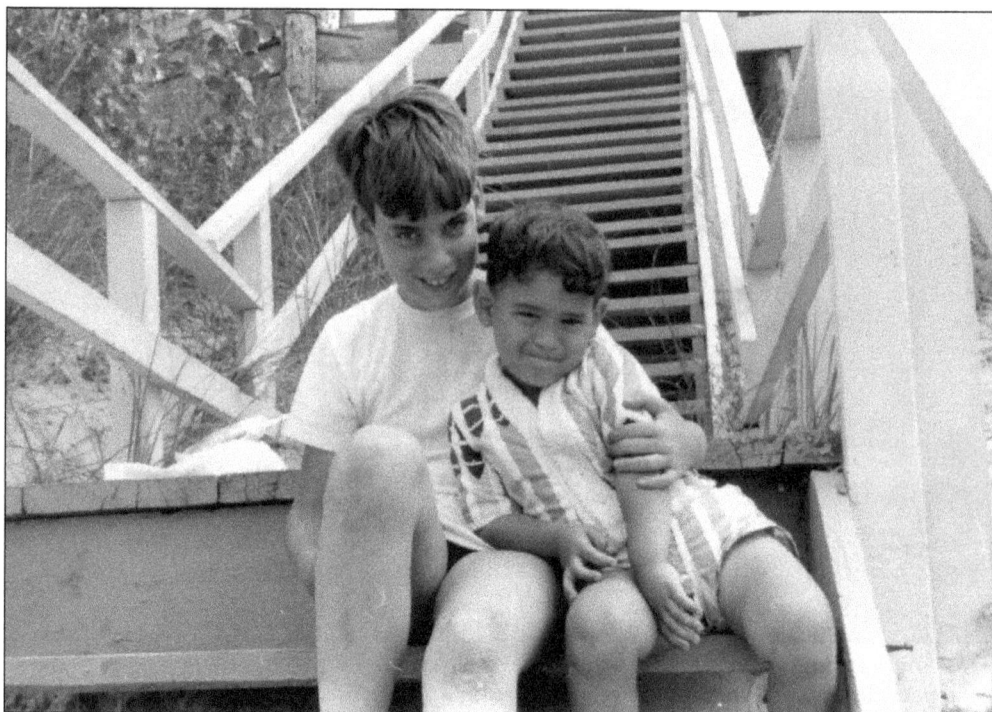

Jimmy Misch and Ralph Rosenberg pose on the Michiana beach stairs in 1967.

Heavily-wooded lots and log-cabin-style siding are characteristics of Michiana's summer homes.

www.ingramcontent.com/pod-product-compliance
Lightning Source LLC
Chambersburg PA
CBHW050630110426
42813CB00007B/1767